Avis Moeller
9353 Harding

WITHDRAWN

D1552184

NOV 0 3 2006

And all was revealed

Columbia College Library
600 South Michigan
Chicago, IL 60605

WITHDRAWN

And all was revealed

LADIES' UNDERWEAR
1907-1980

Doreen Caldwell

ST. MARTIN'S PRESS
NEW YORK

Copyright © Doreen Caldwell, 1981

Designed and produced by Antony Atha
Publishers Ltd, 1 Strafford Road,
Twickenham, Middlesex TW1 3AD.

For information, write:
St. Martin's Press, Inc.,
175 Fifth Avenue, New York, N.Y. 10010.

All rights reserved. No part of this
publication may be reproduced, stored
in a retrieval system, or transmitted,
in any form or by any means, electronic,
mechanical, photocopying, recording
or otherwise, without prior permission
of the copyright owner.

Library of Congress Catalog Card
No: 81-50510
ISBN 0 312 03613 2

Printed and bound in Spain by
Mateu Cromo Artes Graficas, S.A.
Pinto, Madrid

CONTENTS

INTRODUCTION

When I was a child my grandmother used to entrance me with accounts of what she had worn when she was young. Button boots, tucked bodices and caped coats I could understand, but what on earth were camisoles and chemises?

I also remember discovering the two separate halves of long pink stays. Why, I wondered, did they have two separate fastenings – hooks and eyes down what I mistakenly took for the back and holes with laces down the front? Later I found out that some ladies wore combinations under their corsets. This was really puzzling – how on earth did they go to the loo?

This book therefore is largely the outcome of satisfying my childish curiosity about underclothes. There are, of course, omissions; the little contraption of hankies and ribbon that Caresse Crosby stitched together in 1914 in order to uplift her breasts and ease herself from her armour-like corset; the rubber wrap-around belt of the twenties which compressed the buttocks and, in one case at least, was reported to have fused itself to its wearer as she warmed her posterior, skirts uplifted, by the fire. There are no peephole bras, no dancing knickers, few embroidered stockings and no lacy stocking tops. Yet I hope that everyone will recognise some old favourite or abomination.

Although histories of underwear say a great deal about the actual garments, it is often difficult to work out the order in which they were worn. This book is my solution to the problem. I have tried to show how different groups of underclothes could be chosen and the order in which they were put on. Again it has been impossible to include everything. For example, the Edwardian lady is not, alas, wearing her knicker linings.

One obvious effect of underwear and in particular corsetry, is to impose a shape on the wearer. Looking at the drawings in corset advertisements I saw an idealized version of what the garment was supposed to do for its wearer. The ladies illustrated bore their tortures with such ease and elegance that it seemed as though their bodies exactly accorded with the corsets that they wore. This was not the case. However, it would have been misleading to draw girls in ill-fitting corsets which either sagged or caused the flesh to bulge hugely above and below, because I wanted to illustrate the type of figure a woman was aiming at – or that fashion said she should aim at – at a particular point in time. The last picture in each set represents this ideal – and in all probability is almost as unrealistic a shape as those shown in the old fashion advertisements!

What is particularly interesting and curious is the way women have so frequently changed their silhouette. Before 1914 ladies chose to exaggerate their curves, in the twenties they chose to obliterate them. During the thirties they squared their shoulders over slender hips but by the end of the forties the hour-glass shape returned. The close of the fifties saw women as assorted geometric shapes, whilst the sixties culminated in a pair of long legs topped by a short flared tunic.

The cynic would say that these changes were the means by which the fashion industry forced women to spend money. Another argument is that change is born of boredom; but it is facile to dismiss all women as either so bored or so gullible.

I think that with hindsight, it is possible to make broad interpretations about changes in fashion and sum them up as typical images of a period. The fashionably dressed woman represents the look of her time. One can go further and say that rapid, even violent, shifts in shape reflect not only women's attitude towards their role in society and their sexuality, but also mirror the political and international upheavals that have taken place, particularly in the twentieth century. It is probably unwise to take this theory too seriously, but it is interesting how often it can be proved. For example, that instrument of change the corset, is tight-laced during periods of strong currency and authoritative government and thrown in the dustbin when money is bad and promiscuity rampant.

Of course, the fashionable form has been dramatically affected by technological advances in the design of underclothes. The introduction of man-made fibres caused a revolution. Lacing, boning, heavy and exotic fabrics and tedious laundry work have all been abolished. Underwear is lighter, more comfortable, more easily cared for than ever before. Corsets and lingerie are no longer a testimony to a needlewoman's art, nor are they proof of a lady's wealth and status. In 1981 both duchess and shop assistant can choose to buy their underwear from the same chain store.

The sociology of underwear is fascinating but one must not read too much into a pair of silky knickers. Any attempt to become serious is quickly dispelled by reading advertisers' copy which is often more entertaining than the garments themselves.

'. . . knickers which the up-to-date maiden delights in' 1908 . . .'new bloom in petalled lace' 1980 and when the writer is in earnest the effect can be hilarious: 'Pretty knickers are an attractive feature of a trousseau . . . The smallest number of knickers in a trousseau should be two dozen. If pink, blue and yellow suit you best by all means adopt them. Pink is a splendid washing colour and a generally becoming one.' 1903.

It is difficult to write about underwear sensibly. Deliciously pretty clothes demand deliciously pretty prose and the vocabulary is limited. Consequently there is little difference between the descriptions of 1907 and 1981. Yet they are seldom boring because they contain a suggestion of eroticism. Consider these advertisements for constricting pantie-girdles which promise to . . . 'caress you' . . . 'hold you gently but firmly' . . . or 'give you the control you really need'. And the brassiere which 'instead of forcing you just takes you, supports you and softens you.'

1907
The Art of Suggestion

In Edwardian times women clothed themselves in an aura of veiled and beautiful mystery. Whilst carefully, even prudishly, concealing their naked bodies beneath layers of underwear, they developed the art of seduction by suggestion to great heights and it was these very underclothes that formed the basis of their art.

Although it was permissible, desirable, even 'quite fascinating' to reveal the seduction of frills beneath one's dress skirts, a fashion journal of the day warned that '. . . one of the most disastrous aspects of the raised skirt is when the silk underskirt is caught higher than the transparency and reveals . . . . well . . . anything there is to be seen.'

Only a mature woman could wear the fashions of the day to advantage.

The camisole or, as it was now called, the corset-cover, was made of thin silk *en princesse* with practically no sleeves. Because traditional seams were lumpy they were replaced by sewing onto each edge the most minute line of open work insertion. The top of the petticoat was made plain and tight fitting so as not to disturb the smoothness of the hips.

A typical and very expensive garment was this petticoat in rose-coloured silk. It had a long upper skirt whose deep scalloped edges went over an accordion pleated flounce. Whilst the curves of each scallop were trimmed with pale pink chiffon ruching, the points were decorated with lover's knots of cherry ribbon.

The appeal of these seductive garments became audible with their suggestive frou-frou.

'We must all frou-frou until we can't frou-frou any more.'

One or two white muslin petticoats with flounces of *broderie anglaise* and baby ribbon edgings were worn beneath these 'beautiful persuasions' of satin or taffeta. In wintry weather the soft comforting warmth of an extra lace trimmed petticoat would be sought.

'As I knew my frillies were all right I hammocked and it was lovely.'
Eleanor Glyn, *The Visits of Elizabeth*

Drawers became known as knickers, which were wider than ever.

'Wide-leg knickers of Mull muslin or silk with flounce and three rows of insertion, threaded with baby ribbon, worn under lace or silk petticoat for those who like a froth of frillies beneath their dress skirts.'
Fashion Journal

Many ladies still wore their knickers beneath their corset: a custom that survived from early Victorian days when the corset was worn on top of all other underwear and immediately below the outer garment. However, this fashion became impossible as increasingly knickers, like those illustrated, were closed along the centre seam that included the crotch.

What mattered in a lady's figure was the upright poise of the shoulders, a long sloping bust with a straight front line – no hint must be given that the bosom is composed of two breasts – and the graceful curve of the dress over the hips.

A corset for wearing under tailor-made frocks in white coutille, 1906.

All corsets were laced at the back and it was this lacing that did the damage.

'In actuality the abdomen had ceased to exist, all the fullness being thrown upward into the chest and stomach. The waist was excessively narrow and there was a violent bend in the body at the back. About this time there was a considerable outcry against the corset on health grounds: and so formidable was the array of hostile medical opinion that some countries began to legislate against corsets forbidding them altogether for the use of growing girls.' James Laver, *Taste and Fashion*

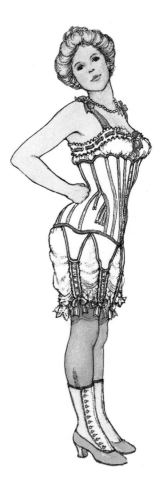

The days of combinations were now past, or so the fashion journals wrote. Everyone wore chemises, Empire pattern, sloped at the waist and tied with coloured bows at the shoulders.

Women rationalised a desire for luxurious underclothes by advocating delicate hygiene. The truly fastidious woman had to ensure that she wore linings within her corset and knickers that could be changed daily, for this dainty underwear with its burden of baby ribbon and lace was more difficult to wash than the 'durable longcloth' worn by the lower classes.

Embroidered silk stockings were delicately tinted to blend with the rest of the chosen ensemble.

Doctors condemned the use of garters as being liable to produce varicose veins.

Through the deliciously silky frills and swirling froths of lingerie and the tight-laced strictures of the corset, women contrived a silhouette whose ideal was epitomised by The Gibson Girl, a creation of the American illustrator Charles Dana Gibson. In London Miss Camille Clifford, England's Gibson Girl sang,

'If you want to lead the fashion
In an independent whirl,
Walk with a bend in your back
And they'll call you a Gibson
                                            Girl,'

Yet, though both corset and lingerie created the fashionable sway-back figure, perhaps the true seductive implication of their lacy luxury is contained in words addressed to a bride:

'Lingerie is by far the most important part of the trousseau.'

1912
The Suffragettes and their Shackles

The fashions of 1912 were resplendently colourful, as if the strong reds, greens, oranges and sulphur yellows were meant to match their wearers' strident demands for emancipation. Yet the line was curiously Oriental; the narrow skirt more fitted for the harem than liberation. The sight of a fashionably dressed militant in the tightest of tight skirts, demanding the vote, provides a beautiful example of irrational contradiction.

But it could be argued that the fashions reflected a desire for equality. For the first time for a hundred years women wore gowns which frankly revealed their anatomical outline. They no longer wanted to seduce with the swish of a petticoat, and by the mystery of suggestion but were eager to be recognised for themselves.

Between the years 1910–14 wide skirts were abandoned for ones so narrow they shackled the legs. After nearly a hundred years of enormously exaggerated hips and tiny waists this was something of a revolution and its immediate effect was a drastic reduction in the number and the elaboration of petticoats. Beneath the tight skirt there was simply no room for them. The line of the petticoat became almost tubular but some, like this simple satin jupon, had accordion pleating, falling in shallow Van Dykes from knee level.

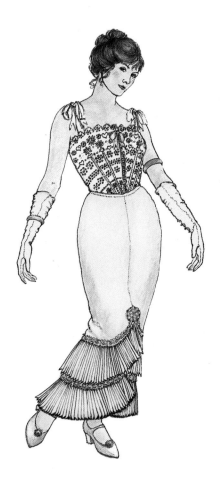

Because the corset was by now so short above the waist, the bust lacked support and so ladies often preferred the security of a boned 'cache-corset' instead of the soft little camisole. It was made of *broderie anglaise* and held in place by ribbon shoulder-straps; the first appearance of an element in feminine underwear that has persisted to this day.

As the skirt narrowed the wide frilly-legged 'French' knickers of the previous decade became impossible to wear. Skirt knickers, which looked for all the world like 18th century knee breeches, were adopted and, since the ladies craved to be clad in French words, these were sometimes known as *culottes*.

'. . . of satin, prettily trimmed with insertion and ribbon flowers at the knee.' *Advertisement*

On the lady's feet 'the white buckskin slipper triumphs'. *Fashion Journal, 1912*

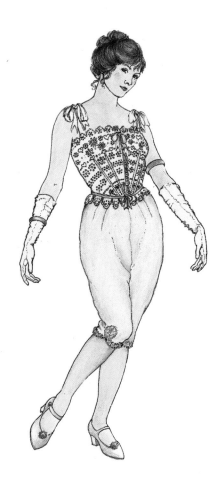

'The corset makes the Figure . . .'

'. . . the contour of the season's figure gives the effect of the natural waist which simulates both the Grecian and the Oriental – with long lines and a slightly curved but confined hip . . .' *Fashion Journal, 1912*

Boning was all important as the strain on the garment was immense. But in 1912 clock spring steel, covered with hard rubber or celluloid became generally adopted, and the whale bone industry never recovered.

This casing of cloth and steel remained straight-fronted, whilst steadily shortening above the waist and descending almost to the knee below. *Punch* joked that year that corsets were so long that they could be buttoned under the instep and the nickname 'spat-corset' was born.

The corset illustrated is the 'Nuform' Weingarten Bros, 1911.

The stockings are the colour of ivory and made from the finest silk, but other colours were available.

'All up-to-date lingerie boasts of broad threaded ribbon while insertion and lace decorate the borders.' *The Lady*

'Summer combinations outline the figure with admirable accuracy.' *Trade Catalogue, 1911*

Although one fashion journal found it 'more amusing than words can describe to observe how frequently the fashion is ignored' these skin-fitting garments helped to create a slender illusion.

Combinations like many of the knickers of this period remained open at the crotch. This opening which started just below the waist at the front and continued to a similar point at the back, was so long that the legs of the garment were almost separated. It was, however, purely practical, for closed combinations and knickers, when allied to the restrictions of skirt, petticoat and corset, would have made visiting the 'loo tortuous to say the least.

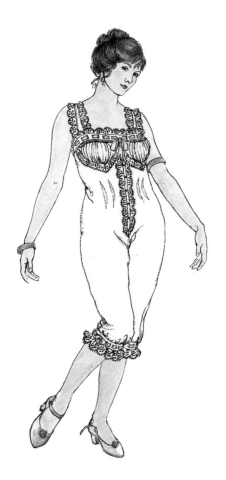

Beneath her bright plumage the lady of 1912 was demure. White, symbol of all that is chaste, was preferred to the excitement of colour. The sensual profusion of frills, flounces and foaming French lace had been rejected for the comparative innocence of *broderie anglaise* and threaded ribbon. In addition although silk and satin still appeared, underclothes were more usually made from lawn, nainsook, stockinette and fine wool. The *Grande Dame* with all her extravagant allurements had been transformed into a much younger and more slender woman whose pure white underwear reflected the milky delicacy of her skin.

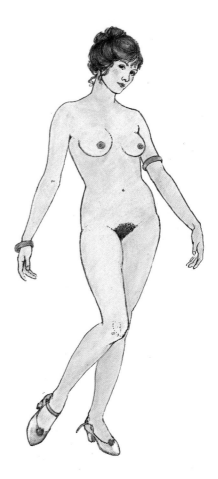

1919
Undies and a New Shape

By the end of the First World War woman was arranging an entirely new shape for herself. Underclothes were no longer designed to emphasise hetero-sexual features but to obliterate them. Every curve was suppressed by the aid of long cylindrical corsets or by a new form of feminine constriction from America which combined hip-belt and bust bodice and was referred to as the 'foundation garment'.

The ideal model was no longer Venus but Ganymede, who now sat waiting, scornful of any of the deliciously suggestive suggestions that had, until recently, surrounded her underwear.

As the harsh realities of war became known underwear became more austere. The short swirling tempestuous petticoats of the early war years were replaced by ones that fell in a gentle fullness, often trimmed with a straight hanging flounce, to just above ankle level. Lingerie as a word, with its associations of French naughtiness, became inappropriate and was replaced by 'Undies'. Yet despite its new nickname and comparative severity it continued to be described in flowery terms by those who wrote for fashion journals.

'Gossamer camisole in Irish-made fine Nainsook daintily embroidered by hand; tiny basque. Value 10/11 White Sale Price 7/11.' *Pontins Advertisement*

'Charming *crêpe de chine* petticoat with underflounce, elaborately embroidered, daintily trimmed Valenciennes, insertion and threaded ribbon: White, Pink and Sky. Value 39/6 White Sale Price 30/-.' *Pontins Advertisement*

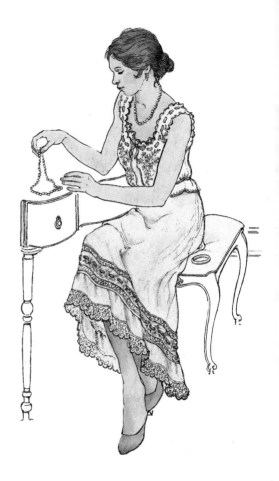

'Irish peasant-made Nainsook knicker, trimmed with an elaborate design, embroidered by hand. This garment has an elastic waist. Value 12/11 White Sale Price 8/6.'
Pontins Advertisement

Eroticism was no longer terribly important, layers of homely looseness served as insulation and protection rather than gift wrapping.

Although black was usual for day-time wear, some girls like Gudrun and Ursula Brangwen in D. H. Lawrence's *Women in Love* chose coloured stockings to complement their dress.

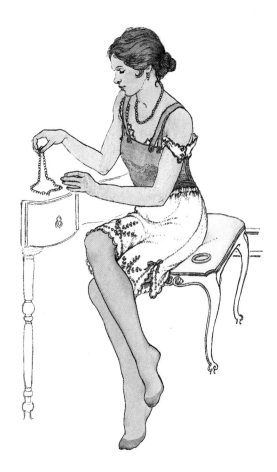

The mannequins who displayed Fashion's Ideals had the physical perfections of the moment, 'such enchanting sexless, bosomless, hipless, thighless, creatures' as a fashion journalist wrote. Such enchantments were naturally beyond the reach of most young women so to simulate the proportions of a young adolescent, curved bodies were bound by long cylindrical corsets which compressed the bust, did nothing for the waist, and successfully obliterated hips and thighs. The corset shown encloses the entire length of the torso. Its power came from the woven elastic material rather than boning, thus it was slightly more comfortable than the cages of cloth and steel of a decade earlier. However, it possessed the disconcerting habit of slipping down or riding up, hence the shoulder straps and suspenders which fulfilled a vital anchoring role.

'Excellent quality chemise in finest Indian longcloth with beautiful hand embroidered design across the front, fastening on the shoulder. Value 10/9 White Sale Price 6/11.'
Pontins Advertisement

Underwear grew more practical and more hygienic during the latter years of the war. Girls could no longer afford the vast wardrobe of silken seductions, trimmed with delicate insertion, ribbon and heavy French lace. Not only were these garments extremely costly, they also required elaborate and expensive laundering. Shortage of money and labour to do the work made them an impossible luxury. A girl now had to have underwear that could easily be washed at home.

The girl of 1920 still clung to some of her older sister's allurements whilst contemplating the charms to be gained from cultivating an adolescent pose. Maybe it was too much to expect her to abandon everything all at once. Perhaps women in search of a new role in society adopted this shape to emphasise their difference; perhaps because austerity made any other role impractical; or was it because these women were at last able to rebel against the idea of being sexual objects, having shown themselves equal to men's work in the war?

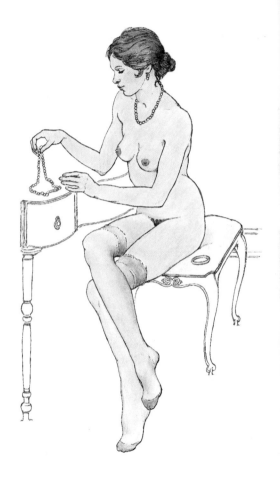

1922
Not Yet a Gentleman

It has been argued that the slaughter of the First World War, which so violently upset the balance of the sexes, resulted in a wave of psychological homosexuality that produced the new boy-girl. True or false, the immediate post-war period found women unwilling to assume their traditional role of housekeeping and motherhood. To demonstrate this and also possibly as a reaction against the old order, they set out determinedly to obliterate their female outline and assume the shape of an immature male.

Although Vita Sackville-West may have sung the praises of breeches and gum boots, for most trousers were unthinkable. Instead girls donned slightly clerical, sack-like robes that just grazed the ankle, defiantly bobbed their hair and publicly powdered their noses.

Approval was not found everywhere. One fashion journal lamented 'One cannot help wishing for a less independent, less hard, more feminine product than the average twentieth century girl'.

28

The long skirts of 1922–4 required that princess petticoats were worn almost to the ankle.

'A princess petticoat in silk milanese, waistline held in with elastic. Length from shoulder 48–51in. Shoulder straps and scalloped hem. Price 35/-.' *Trade Journal*

'Fashion denies us petticoats or any underwear that is not of the flimsiest material.' *Fashion Journal*

In 1920 Government balloon fabric for lingerie was advertised at 3/- per yard.

In 1920 a new item of feminine underwear appeared – cami-knickers – which were formed, as their name suggests, by a joining together of camisole and knickers. At first they were called 'step-ins', because this is how they were put on, but the term was later applied to elastic girdles with side zips.

The cami-knickers illustrated are of *crepe de chine*, the skirt falling in points from an elastic sided waist. The dips in the hem echo the uneven skirts of evening dresses worn in 1922, an echo which occurred again in 1927–8 as the hems of the short skirts swooped down at the back.

Ivory had ousted white as the fashionable underwear shade – perhaps the girl of the early twenties no longer thought of herself as chaste – more probably because of the universal superfluity of khaki dye.

'To disguise the figure is one of the great arts at present . . . . for the new fashion with its irresistible schoolgirl lines.' *Fashion Journal*

To conform, many women were compelled to wear some sort of 'correcting' or flattening garment round the bust. This was almost as ridiculous as the previous fashion which had so viciously reduced the waist.

'Hand-made bust bodice in ivory silk with ribbon shoulder straps and finished with applique embroidery.' *Fashion Journal*

The corset had vanished but the corset belt which had taken its place was worn universally. For the young and slender it ended at the waist. It was usually made from woven porous elastic or *broché* satin with the minimum of boning and for the first time the belt was worn next to the skin.

'Pure silk hose with openwork clocks, feet and hem lined with lisle: Black, white and all fashionable shades. Price 12/11 a pair.' *Fashion Journal*

During the 1920's artificial silk stockings, later known as rayon, gained ground on the pure silk variety for everyday wear. They never took over completely because although they were stronger and cheaper, they were fairly thick and possessed an unflattering shine. Generally they were beige in colour with little variety and there was nothing to match a suntan until the very end of the thirties, when nylon was about to oust both rayon and silk.

In 1923 the fully fashioned, shaped and seamed stocking fought with the seamless version for predominance. The latter looked like pretty, bare legs from a distance. Close to the wrinkles showed – for seamless stockings seldom fitted well over the entire leg.

'The modern girl has ceased to be a woman but has not yet become a gentleman.' So remarked a fashionable preacher in 1922.

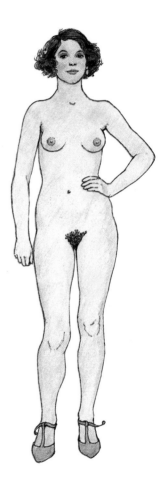

1926
The Bright Young Thing

In the early twenties the dark
haired, beautiful 'Coco' Chanel
came back to Paris with a bronzed
skin and for the first time in history
it was fashionable to be brown. By
the middle of the decade the cult of
the tan had become a religion. This
stimulated cosmetic manufacturers
to produce lotions to prevent
burning, potions to promote
browning and stains to make or fake
it, in addition to the wide variety of
skin foods, powders and other
cosmetics they had begun to
produce a year or so earlier.

It was a brave new industry that
had nothing to do with the old
order. The bright young thing
revelled in its shock. Her painted
face, bared limbs, shorn head and
little girl's frock proclaimed she was
no part of the society that had flung
the world into chaos.

The layers of underclothing were drastically reduced, partly because of the new spirit of equality (bare skin is a great leveller), partly because of the cult of youth (little girls have no need for corsets and lingerie), but mostly because the lack of covering gave a sense of freedom, liberation from the old standards of morality.

In 1924 the chemise became a vest. It ended at hip level and was worn tucked inside the knickers.

'Pure silk milanese vest and pure silk milanese knickers finished at yoke and hem by a band of net and hand embroidered applique. Price 45/6.' *Debenham and Freebody's*

And that was all!

This sprite eschewed further clothing. Near nudity was fun – besides she had no need for compressing or suppressing undergarments. Nature had granted her a straight stick-like little body.

Curiously pink and shiny artificial silk hose rolled round garters above the knee.

An American fashion.

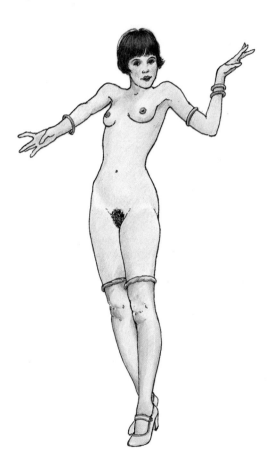

1926
The Camibocker and Combinaire

For those whose silhouette did not contain 'an ineffable suggestion of slender feminine charm' there were starvation diets, exercises and slenderising patent medicines, or, if all else failed, 'a creaseless perfection' acquired 'by wearing the minimum of clothing beneath'. Composite garments which were supposed to fulfil this aim abounded.

The Camibocker, comprising camisole and closed directoire knickers, is one example. It was a modest 'intimate' creation which concealed 'even its smallest edges'. Calls of nature were facilitated by a let down flap at the back, closed with 3 buttons at the waist and 'poppers' down the sides.

The girl with large breasts and round hips had problems, even if her waist was small. 'We must throw away our waist lines' sang one journalist, whilst another announced 'Today we are taught to pull our corsets up in the front and down at the back and so straighten out the figure to emulate once more nature's more delightful, supple, straight form'. In order to compress her buttocks and eradicate her 'high spots' the rounded girl resorted to the *combinaire* in *broché* satin and elastic.

This dreadful garment with its total shapelessness epitomised the feminine ideal of the twenties.

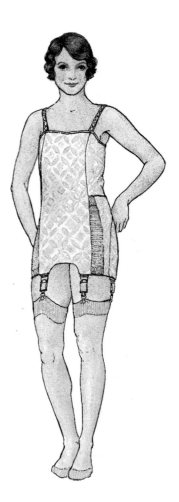

1927
The Perfect Peach

'With boys like this, one could give the girls a miss.' *French Cartoon*

By 1926 the glorification of the boyish figure reached its apotheosis. In an attempt to imitate the proportions of the adolescent male, young women struggled to obliterate their breasts and reduce their hips by drastic slimming. With their eyebrows torn out supposedly to reveal the beauty of their eyes and increase the symmetry of their features, their hair sleekly shingled, and all facial expression hidden under a mask of cosmetics, the school-boyish girl frantically blasted her way through to the benefits of emancipation. It was a feverish reaction against the decaying ideas of the old social system.

'It is almost impossible to imagine anything more fascinating than the lingerie of today. The cami-knicker at its best is a thing of sheer delight in peach-coloured georgette with guaging at the hips and satin bindings.' *Eve*

The cami-knicker may not seem a particularly seductive garment but by modern standards it might be judged indecent. Its only claim to be a 'knicker' was a thin strip of material which passed between the legs, catching the hem together at the front and back. It is therefore no wonder that a contemporary journalist exclaimed, 'Just about anything might be seen!', when a short skirted flapper sat down and crossed her legs.

In 1926 the Separate Brassiere appeared. Although it bore a marked resemblance to the Bust Improver, its purpose was to squash rather than enhance the breasts.

A new 'non-support', an elastic, rubber and satin suspender belt, was worn round the minute buttocks. It ignored the waist but kept the flesh coloured silk stockings stretched tightly over the legs. In the mid-twenties seductive lingerie disappeared as 'amusing undies' took over.

'Undies that helped create 'tube figures for tube frocks' were almost devoid of sexual attraction. But girls still needed to feel desirable and this erotic instinct was expressed by their taste for colour. White, the traditional symbol of the pure and chaste, fell from popularity. Although this was partly due to the improved methods of dyeing washable fabrics, coloured underwear would not have been produced without demand. The bright flapper could hug herself in the knowledge that she seemed a perfect peach in peach-coloured undies, and as exotic as a hothouse bloom in cami-knickers of orchid pink.

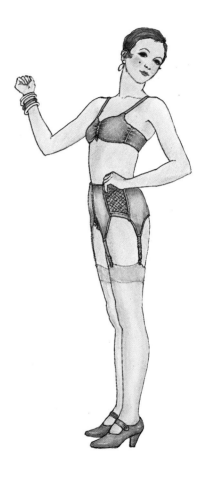

Stockings had to be silk, or at least artificial silk, and flesh coloured. They were expensive; never before had so much money been spent on women's leg coverings.

Since breasts, hips and buttocks were out the young men of the day turned their attention to the only attraction left. An erotic aesthetic arose based on the newly discovered seductiveness of the feminine leg clothed in tight flesh coloured silk stockings.

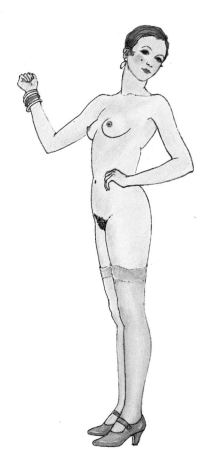

1929
The Feminine Form is Lovely

By the end of the twenties it had been legs, legs, legs for the last five years. Then, either through boredom, or because girls longed to hide their often imperfect limbs; because the cloth manufacturers complained that short skirts brought short profits, or just for the sake of fashion's predictable caprice, hem lines fell and attention switched to other parts of the female form.

One woman's magazine exclaimed 'Fashion's new discovery that the feminine form is lovely'. While another wrote 'Once more you are to look feminine, really feminine this time with graceful curves, a natural waistline and longer skirts'.

'The straight sack-like slip is wrong . . . Slips are shaped like the frock and fit the natural waist.'
Trade Journal

This hand-made slip in flowered *crêpe de chine* and trimmed with ecru lace, which was immensely popular that year, has a brassiere top and side opening. Some slips also had a shaped band at the waist to which knickers were attached, thus, as the advertisement said, 'combining the three garments especially for the evening' although it was unfashionable to wear more than brassiere and panties after dark beneath one's outer finery.

'With the very short skirt, knickers confined at the knee were necessary, but now skirts are longer and slimness just as much admired, the best type of knicker, often yoked, ends at the knee without gathers (or if of silk tricot in a garter band). Flowered *crêpe de chine* is favoured for day wear.' *The Lady*

In 1929 little mention was made of breasts but their presence was recognised by corset makers. The tube-like *combinaire* now sported two breast pockets, that compressed rather than improved by uplift. The bosom had only made a timid reappearance.

A year later acknowledgements were bolder. One manufacturer promised that in his new corset every type of figure had been studied – a model designed to meet every need. Since his advertisement also mentions 'graceful curves' and 'a feminine line' it can be concluded that he included the breasts.

Variety too had increased, advertisements spoke of 'corselettes, wrap-arounds and step-ins for day wear' and for the evening 'the daintiest imaginable shadow garments'.

The foundation garment illustrated combines a lace bodice with a pink rayon and elastic panelled hip belt. It has a side opening and is equipped with six suspenders and striped elastic shoulder straps. These new 'Corselettes' gently moulded the figure rather than pushed and pulled it up, in and out.

'Pure silk hose with lisle tops and feet in black, white and all fashionable shades @ 5/11 a pair.'
Advertisement

'Lisle thread' was a pseudonym for cotton, and considering the price of this lady's hose it is probable that her thighs and feet are clothed in elegantly luxurious words alone.

Hips had still to be slim. Slimming and slenderness were in. The siren of the late 1920's had no intention of returning to the endless pregnancies of her mother's generation in which wide child-bearing qualities reigned supreme.

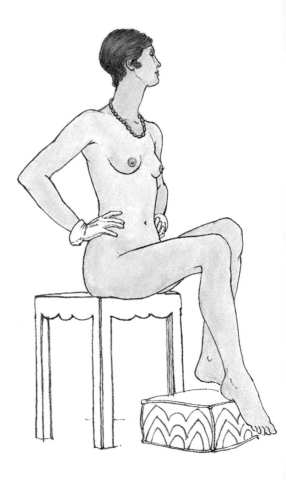

1933
Smart, Sleek and Sexy

By 1933 women had turned their backs on the frivolities of the twenties. Flappers were out and the Garbo look was in. Perhaps because so many girls had to look for work during the depression, fashion ordained an alert competent figure with square shoulders and slim straight hips. For those without these attributes shoulder pads were a help gratefully and universally received.

But if a young woman looked mannish by day, in the evening it was another matter. The longer skirts shifted the emphasis from the legs to the back. Backs were bared to the waist and skirts drawn tightly over the hips to reveal the shape of the tightly curved buttocks. A new erogenous zone had been discovered.

'Each glided past with her suspenders as apparent under her skin tight skirt as if she had been wearing them outside.' *Journalist reporting on a Fashion Show*

47

Decolletage had reappeared for the first time in 25 years, but at the back. However breasts, albeit two small timidly curved bumps, also came back into fashion.

'It is important in this season of revealing lines to have a slip that fits like paper on the wall.' *Advertisement*

A backless princess petticoat with the new adjustable satin ribbon straps in Chartreuse satin and needle-run lace.

'The skirt is cut on the cross to cling the better.' *Advertisement*

The fabrics used for underwear were becoming more heavily luxuriant.

'Chartreuse satin knickers that conform to the figure.' *Advertisement*

Although one was permitted to show almost anything except one's ankles by evening, it was vital that almost everything was 'slim as a Maypole'. This entailed under-clothing that was 'a mere nothing to wear' and 'just a caress'. If you were unfortunate enough not to be endowed with the highest standards of natural proportions, then under your clinging unlined satin dress, you were condemned to . . .

The 2-way stretch all-in-one corset and brassiere which supplied the sculptured foundation on which the tightly fitting dress appeared moulded. This model made by Warner Bros Corsets Ltd was made from Lastex, a fine elastic thread that could be woven into a fabric. It had a specially designed system of straps so that nothing passed across the back above the waist. Six suspenders strap down that portion of the naked thigh above the stocking tops, to ensure that at least two fascinating and tempting bumps were visible beneath the clinging skirt.

Perhaps the memory of veiled
nudity spurred on the desirous
gentleman as he fought to remove
his loved one's resisting roll-on, or
maybe he delighted in her contorted
wriggling and emergent swellings as
she struggled out of this elasticised
sheath.

1937
A Superb Piece of Sculpture

By the mid-thirties the retreat from the exhibitionism of the twenties was complete. Noise, caprice and indecorous behaviour had been replaced by refinement, discretion and good breeding. By day the line was square shouldered and severely tailored; by night there were constant, if half-hearted, attempts at Victorian revivals.

The ideal beauty was a glamorously groomed woman of a certain age, whose elegant figure was gently supported by light, flexible and easily laundered corsetry. Underneath there was luxury. Her aristocratic good taste dictated that she considered hand-made, beautifully cut, clinging lace trimmed lingerie in satin and *crêpe de chine* as normal.

'It is no longer smart to be sleek, slick and sexy but smart to be feminine in a new calm way showing the body as a superb piece of sculpture.' *Vogue*

'Enchanting and deliciously feminine cami-knickers in *crêpe suzette* or satin of sheath-like fit. Pink or peach. Price 21/9.'
Advertisement

'Breasts are worn high and pointed to an astonishing degree. . . .'

'The Kestos "Handkerchief" bra in chiffon and black lace.'

. . . While the diaphragm must be flatter than flat.'

'A very light, inexpensive flexible roll-on in pink Lastex yarn. Price 12/6.' *Advertisement*

The pursuit of physical perfection, the growing interest in sports and the desire for graceful beauty led to an enormous improvement in the quality and range of corsetry available. Most notable among which was a pair of very brief, very light and flexible elastic trunks – the forerunner of the 'pantie-girdle' that appeared in the sixties.

'Legs, though no longer so wildly exciting as in the Naughty Nineties, still have the power to charm.' *Advertisement*

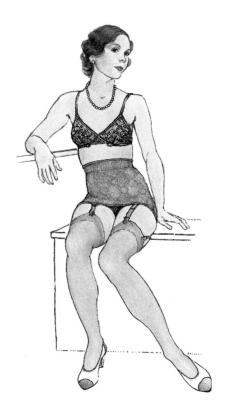

The thirties have been seen as a time when women were beginning to seek out femininity without sacrificing their new won liberties. Whatever the case this fashionable society of French windows, good manners, tennis, grand pianos, Hollywood glamour, Noel Coward and Gertrude Lawrence obscured the rise of fascism in Germany.

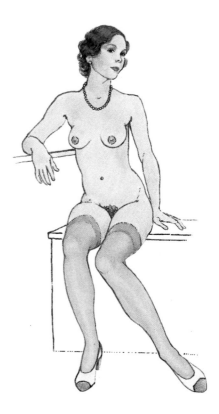

1939
Restraints and Rendez-Vous

At the time of the Munich crisis, women dressed themselves in an odd mixture of crinolines, leg o' mutton sleeves and ridiculously small sprouting hats. In the full skirts and corseted waists a new conception of woman and the end of the 'woman-as-comrade' ideal, which had reigned since the end of the First World War, could be seen.

'The new woman must be mysterious, alluring and witty. . . . She will be vested and gloved and corseted . . . there must be frou-frou and femininity, restraints and *rendez-vous*.'

'There is a delicious excitement about these new clothes, for in them woman is rediscovering herself, her personality and her sex.'

'The era of varnished chic is over: modernity is quite dead. Grandmother was right . . . she concentrated on slimming her waist . . .' *Vogue* 1938–39

A swinging petticoat in triple ninon* with frilled lace at the lower edge, which as a fashion editor of the time said 'Looks perfectly sweet, showing just an inch below your frock.'

* Ninon was a type of voile that was widely used in the early '20's and before the First World War. Between 1925–1939 there had been a great improvement in the quality, variety and availability of man-made fibres and by the mid 30's they predominated in the manufacture of underclothes. The fact that an old fashioned natural fabric appears in 1939 is perhaps an indication of the wish to end 'the era of varnished chic'.

'Camisoles have made a successful comeback.'

An 'enchanting frilly for the tiny lady' in triple ninon, trimmed with delicate lace and broad threaded satin ribbon, 'of muted pastel shades and white'. *Advertisement*

58

'Giving the Game Away.'

But the Game's up unless you have the new figure – the figure of eight – which the new clothes demand: so get it by hook, by crook or by corset!'

'Boned corset in pink satin with up-lift brassiere.' *Advertisement*

This lady's 'Figure of eight' could be closely associated with those times of unshakeable and honourable solidarity, the golden age of the Edwardian era. Outwardly and inwardly she played the little woman 'the tiny lady', who by lacing in her curves expressed a desire, albeit an unconscious one for protection.

'Add bloomers by way of bravado.'

This extraordinary garment, designed by Lachasse, was not generally worn but its inclusion helps to illustrate the widely unstable fashions of 1938–39. There was no look, no universal line – women appeared in costumes that seemed to have come from an odd assortment of dressing up boxes rather than from the houses of *haute couture*.

Garters in black lace and satin ribbon to intrigue.

'Stockings as seductive as the first stir of temptation; in service sheers 4/11, 6/11 and Sansheen chiffon 4/11 to 12/6 a pair.' *Advertisement*

Stockings were no longer prohibitively expensive.

1943
Utility-Futility

In 1941 the Government introduced clothes rationing and fashion almost died. The meagre portion of coupons dealt out hardly covered the most basic essentials, and women were forced to wear the clothes they already possessed. In 1942 Utility garments were introduced and the clothing industry was regimented. Because of the strict limitation imposed on the amount of material used the same short boxy silhouette was seen everywhere. Rayon stockings were almost unobtainable, so girls took to wearing slacks in winter in spite of objections from conservative employers.

But amid all the austerity sex appeal bloomed. Driven to find other means of expression the face, head and bosom became the focus of attention.

'The Gardenia Look'
'Smooth foundation lotion over cherry coloured cream rouge, fluff on cameo powder and complete the picture with cherry lipstick, green eyeshadow and mascara. For allure add nail varnish and scent. . . .'
Fashion Journal

All were essential for every self-respecting girl in the autumn of 1940 when men were fighting the Battle of Britain.

Extraordinary pains were taken over the most elaborate long and frizzy-fringed hair-do's and the Government was compelled to issue the safety slogan 'Be in Fashion – Cover Your Hair', to girls who worked in factories.

Brassieres were the most important item of dress. If they were unobtainable they were constructed from triangular pieces of cotton, lengths of tape and elastic.

Pink rayon-satin Utility cami-knickers worn over pink cotton Kestos-type bra.

Women grumbled that Utility roll-ons did nothing for the figure. One journalist groaned 'Where can one buy good corsets and brassieres – Nowhere!' The label Utility was nicknamed Futility. But roll-ons could not be worn easily. Without stockings to anchor them they rolled up.

As stockings were scarce women either wore socks or took to covering their legs with make-up, suntan lotion and even a concoction of cocoa and water, and drawing lines down the back to imitate seams.

With the enforced length of leg displayed lacking the silky allure of stockings, breasts became objects of irresistible desire; while the mouth, that other erotic centre of the age, had the 'red badge of courage' painted on every lip – even if it was only in beetroot juice.

At one stage it was reported that some factory girls were protesting that they could not win the war without the help of brassieres and lipstick.

1949
The New Look

No other Paris collection has ever had or ever will have the emotional impact of Dior's 'New Look' of 1947. The skimpy short skirts of the war years were swept aside by long, fully-skirted, curved shoulder clothes created from yards of material. Voices were raised in outrage. French women screamed that while some paid extravagant sums for dresses their children went without milk; in Britain it was rumoured that the Government would regulate the length of women's skirts, whilst in America there were protests that 'in this age of hardship the New Look would widen the gulf between the classes'.

But this reaction was beside the point. The New Look fulfilled a deep need in the women of the world who after the war years longed to be women again.

Dior transformed the female silhouette into an hourglass with its high rounded bust, tiny waist emphasised by hip padding and abundant skirts which ended just twelve inches above the ground. It was a gesture of nostalgia for the security of the Edwardian age.

'Beautifully cut camisole combining brassiere in white silk crepe trimmed with hand made lace and ribbon insertion.
Matching waist petticoat, full and flounced.' *Advertisement*

The underwear generally available was not alluring. Any pretty lingerie that was advertised was astronomically priced and indistinguishable from that which had been produced in the thirties.

'There is a fashion for showing the edge of one's lace lavished petticoat below the hem of one's skirt.' *Vogue*

'Knickers in white silk crepe, slim and well cut trimmed with hand made lace, elastic at the waist.'
Advertisement

Prices were not quoted on advertisements, presumably because the cost was of little consequence to those who could afford to buy.

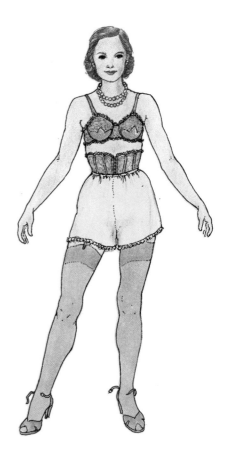

'The new tall willow look is a matter for the brassiere' *Vogue*

And the new high rounded bosom quite often a matter of 'Shaplies', British mass produced false busts made of sponge rubber. Coupon free. Price 10/6

Minute waist lines were essential so women took to waist-clinching waspies.

French *guêpière* and brassiere in embroidered grey muslin mounted on pink silk.

Ordinary mortals without money or coupons had to make do with waspies constructed from cotton, elastic and clock-spring steel.

'Stockings for the Sheerer Era. Sheer silk fully fashioned stockings in all shades of brown: Price 23/- a pair and 3 coupons.' *Advertisement*

Nylon stockings were the one innovation. Coveted for their sheer silky luxury the first ones were vastly expensive and they became synonymous with the Black Market.

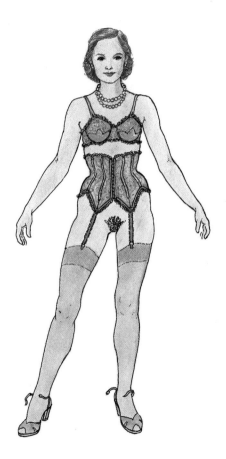

In Britain certainly the New Look did not last although a full skirted shape with nipped-in waist survived in ordinary summer dresses for almost the next ten years. Shortages, rationing and expense simply ruled it out. It was a mirage of lotus eating luxury which only the rich could obtain. The poverty of underclothing beneath the romantic outer coverings adversely affected women's attitude towards their dress. It was no use looking presentable when all was drab underneath and soon they were complaining that pretty things were non-existent.

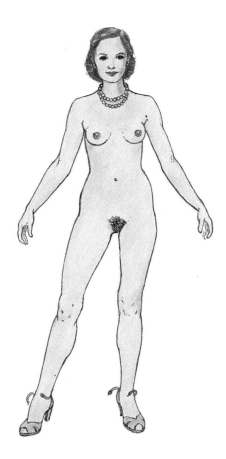

1952
The American Idea

The early fifties was a time of control. In Britain clothes and sweets were still rationed while in America the Communist witch hunts of McCarthy induced a mood of conformity. This feeling was reflected in fashion. No longer were the magazines full of pictures of pretty women in pretty frocks, instead they were full of corsetry advertisements. And what corsetry! 'American inspiration' produced miracles of scientifically constructed elastic and nylon diagonal controls and diamond panels, which, it was claimed, removed the necessity of muscular control, and control was good when exercised without violence.

'Austerity and the Lady-Like Line' '. . . away with the euphoria of the New Look and the fripperies of yesteryear. The new essential of fashion is that it should be discreet.' Christian Dior, *Dior by Dior*

'. . . a selection of underthings for you to take to the root of your wardrobe . . . to make you feel good all the way through.

A beautifully cut nylon tricot slip – double flounced and edged with nylon net and lace. Pink or white. Price £2:19:11.' *Vogue*

The beauty of this slip lies not so much in its appearance but in its beautifully tailored fit facilitated by adjustable shoulder straps.

'Nylon tricot pantees, trimmed with nylon net and lace. Elastic at waist and leg.' *Advertisement*
Nylon, the miracle fabric, made from a mixture of coal and water and used for ropes, nets and conveyor belts was hardly the stuff to quicken the romantic heart.

A Kempat K Bra, whose 'diagonal control gives beauty of uplift and freedom of movement in a degree hitherto unknown. In cotton and elastic.' *Advertisement*

'All corsetry has the American idea.' *Vogue*

'American nylon power net with panels of satin lastique. Diamond panels whose sheer magic slims down the figure. Four magical strips of elastic give perfect muscular control and support in absolute comfort. An inimitable American design that does away with bulges and rolls without pinch or poke.' *Advertisement*

Inspired by Paris, styled in New York and presented in London this pink nylon step-in corset allowed its wearer to move as she willed whilst promising never to ride up her elegantly flat behind. The 'Nu-Back's' secret lay in its two independently constructed and securely boned overlapping back panels, whose overlap increased or diminished as the wearer bent and stretched.

'Something lovely to wear under your strapless sheath dress in nylon lace not for export . . . This cobwebby nylon lace makes our new bra a dream of daintiness. Brief princess style. Elastic under bust. In nylon, taffetas and lace. Pink and ecru. Front fastening too. Price 27/6.'
English Rose Advertisement

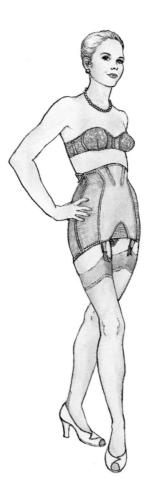

Line was all important, but the line must be severely and properly womanly. Bosoms were uplifted, often with the help of judiciously placed pads of foam rubber, and panties, which created their own disordered bumps and ridges under close fitting skirts, were not infrequently worn beneath the girdle or even discarded altogether. Although encased in a skin tight dress and properly bound by bra and girdle the absence of pants gave the young woman of the fifties a deliciously secret sense of freedom.

1952
Erotic Engineering

Evening alone retained an element of romance. Tempestuous petticoats, tiny waists and voluptuous bosoms were whirled round dance floors. Construction and austerity were forgotten. Dior was still the leader of fashion and was reported to like his women, soft, very feminine, with plump cheeks, dark and smiling.

At a time when pretty clothes were hard to find evening petticoats fulfilled a great need. Their hems were usually buoyed out by several layers of stiffened muslin and ruffled taffeta and in the desire to appear 'bewitchingly lovely' girls wore them inside out so that when they sat down their legs emerged from a tantalising corolla of frothy frills. It was a clever simulation of seductive luxury.

This extraordinary garment, comprising two woven plastic hoops held in place with tapes, is a crinoline. Like the cage crinolines of the 1860's it was a cheap and effective way of puffing out the skirt. Yet despite its romantic name this contraption was not a thing of beauty nor was it easy to wear. The trouble with these lightweight suspensions was that they could be unexpectedly and disconcertingly revealing, not only when sitting but also when walking – especially on a breezy evening.

The crinoline was not for everyday wear.

'"Pantees" from a set of "Exquisite Undies" in pink *crêpe de chine* and black lace. Price £10:2:6 for slip and pants.' *Advertisement*

'Plaza sheers make beauty a duty.' *Advertisement*

80

'Strapless plunged brassiere, top welded to alternating panels of nylon and fine elastic. Strategically boned with back fastening. Price 18 guineas.'

This copy which appeared in a review in *Vogue* seems more fitted to a solidly designed piece of machinery than a description of a garment associated more normally with erotic fantasies. Perhaps in this age of austerity the reviewer was embarrassed by the prohibitive cost.

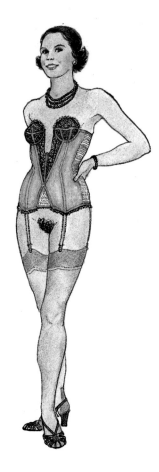

Nylon may not have been the stuff romantic heroines chose but nylons were. Their fully fashioned cling, their subtly transparent sheen, gave legs a glamorous smoothness which all women quickly came to consider their right. In drab surroundings they held a promise of a Brave New World; but the cost of that promise was still prohibitive.

1956
Teenage Warheads

In 1956 the first exclusively teenage fashions came into being. Bardot and Monroe, the French and the American, vied for predominance. Bosoms were in: the French aimed for the apple shape, and softly padded their bras with foam rubber, whilst the Americans turned breasts into warheads, constructing and reinforcing conical bust cups, whose pointed tips seemed almost to penetrate the tight sweaters then in vogue.

The young spun through the rhythms of rock and roll dressed in the most feminine and fictitiously curved fashions since Edwardian days, with tiny waists, swelling breasts, swirling skirts and underneath the frou-frou petticoat. Every girl wanted to look like Bardot – the same hair style and clothes, the same stilted walk on stiletto heels, and everywhere the same pout and cool saucy stare.

The can-can petticoat in stiffened nylon, so called because a turn *could* produce the sight of a suspender or two. At first stiffened nylon belonged exclusively to the fashion houses, but when in the late '50's it became generally available a myriad airy petticoats floated into the shops and were sold for a fraction of what they had originally cost.

84

Girls often wore an older petticoat under the crisp light new one to give their skirts more buoyancy and to safeguard against showing too much leg as they danced. Stiffened nylon became known as paper nylon because of its tendency to become permanently crumpled with age.

'A really beautiful vest in wool and cotton mixture fully fashioned.'
Advertisement

The vest was still widely worn because of the general lack of central heating, but the teenagers hated it. Its style which had changed little in thirty years epitomised frumpish middle age. Moreover its bulk threatened the carefully contrived silhouette with ruin. Worn over the knickers to preserve a smooth line, the garment rode up and lay in ugly sausage rolls round the waist and hips. A year or two later as skirts narrowed fashion editors were advising their readers to 'do as the models do and tuck your vest inside your girdle'.

'Comfort, freedom and a smooth hipline
Petalena Milanicks wash and iron easily fine rayon milanese.'

Advertisement

In the main what went on underneath the tempestuously petticoated vision was an uninteresting and tatty conglomeration of white cotton, nylon, rubber and elastic.

Despite the burgeoning of breasts the age was still curiously innocent and inhibited. A doctor reported on the way girls had been brought up to think of sex 'as an animal instinct . . . something a nice girl didn't want'. Although petticoat frills were skilfully played, a display of naked thigh above stocking tops was dreaded. Underwear, unless it was French was seldom designed to stimulate desire.

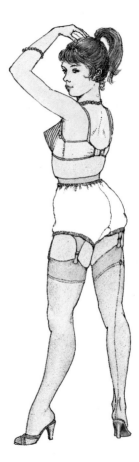

'All American women know beauty begins with a bra. . . .'

'Exquisite Form: Floating Action.'

'As necessary as lipstick: as important as perfume: A good bra is a beauty must. If you have a pretty figure thank your lucky stars and keep it with Exquisite Form.'

'Or do you need their "Equaliser" with its Cunningly Concealed Contours.' *Advertisement*

Although the blatant bearing of vital statistics did not go on in fashionable circles, all became concerned with the cultivation of their mammary glands. The bra became the most advertised item of clothing. For the less well-endowed a lining of latex foam was whirlpool-stitched into the cup to create 'The Equalizer' with its 'cunningly concealed contours' for that 'All, Oh so feminine American look.'

The Playtex Living Girdle

'Absorbent downy soft cotton and figure moulding latex.'
Advertisement

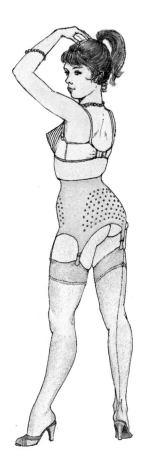

88

American and pink latex rubber produced something particularly nasty and worthy of note since it was almost as heavily advertised as the brassiere. The Living Girdle was a rubber roll-on which promised lithe and lissom freedom but passed a sticky sentence on those who wore it. It is doubtful if it was worn regularly since the action of pulling on and dragging off its flabby adhesiveness demanded the qualities of both martyr and contortionist.

'I want to be simple, wild and sexy.' Brigitte Bardot.

The ideal girl of the mid-fifties was symbolised by a curious mixture of innocence and primitive, physical allure.

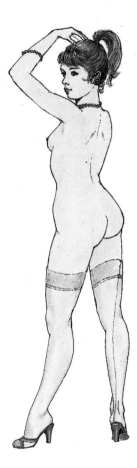

1956
The Mature Sophisticate

By contrast fashion for the older woman was 'carefully sophisticated'; the line had begun to skim the figure. New fabrics, finer and stronger than before, produced sleek, light corsetry and black replaced pink as the primary colour. In the extraordinary way of fashion, pink was no longer French; it had become a joke; sausage pink epitomised all ancient corsetry and the not so ancient too.

'Le soir, pour les femmes, c'est l'heure du charme, de la tendresse et aussi . . . des audaces.' *Elle*

Decorative deep waisted brassieres embracing both ribs and hip bones, called *bustiers* in France and rechristened Merry Widows in England, created long slender torsoes surmounted by the pretty curves of nestling breasts. Whilst *combinés*, all-in-one foundations, were so gossamer that they seemed to one fashion journalist to be less corsets than fitted lingerie.

'Pour Madame: En tricot de nylon et fine dentelle un slip noir, au charme feminin classique.' *French Fashion Journal*

'Slim sheaths, longline princess dresses all demand a silhouette to match: A strong light underlining that's almost like a second skin to wear. . . . This is what the new corsets are doing – a better controlling job – because of the new tense light fabrics and new skilful intricacies of cutting and shaping.'
Vogue

'Cross over bands front and back give a nice moulded torso: light boning smooths the waist: Bra is softly padded and firmly wired underneath: widely spaced detachable straps. Price £4:13:0.'
Caprice

'The world is a hard place. Women must be the smile of the world.'
Christian Dior, *Dior by Dior*

1960
An Elegant Aura

The fashionable woman of 1960 was a smoothly coiffured, casually elegant creature whose deep-set lustrous eyes looked lazily out into a new decade. She was French or possibly Italian. Her figure was supple and soft, her golden legs were enhanced by gracefully curved shoes. She was seductive. It was not so much her look or her line but her aura.

There was a revival too in the importance of lingerie, the word 'undies' was out. In 1958 *The Guardian* wrote 'the most modish exquisitries are completely opaque. It is very unchic to be sheer' and advertisements spoke of 'breathtaking lingerie in shadow proof nylon with the look and feel of pure silk' or lingerie 'lavished with lace at bodice and hem'. All underwear was coloured and although the colours were generally the same as before they were now described as 'dawn pink, wild rose, white gleam, crocus yellow or the vibrant haze of firebird'.

'Exquisite lingerie in nylon brimming with crisp matching lace: Slit skirted both sides. Price 42/6.'
Advertisement

There was a jarring note. Persuaded by its spring morning appearance women purchased a crocus yellow petticoat and then found that no one had produced a yellow bra and girdle to match.

'Crocus yellow nylon tricot pantees. Price 17/6.' *Advertisement*

The inspiration for corsetry came from France and promised gossamery indulgence. Diagonal controls had quietly melted into 'gentle criss-cross bands to flatten you where you most need it'. Brassiere advertisements promised 'an exhilarating sense of comfort and freedom.' As prices tumbled women were encouraged to create a corsetry wardrobe and articles in magazines advocated the purchase of several girdles 'to suit different dress styles'.

'For the young figure. . . .
Brassiere in white nylon lace.
Price 27/6.'

'Take flight from the tyranny of inches. Gentle criss-cross bands flatten you where you most need it. Girdle in blue pearl Lycra. Price 139/6.' *Advertisement*

'in deep suntanned shades . . . *Long Life* nylons can't snag, practically never run: stretch tops.' *Advertisement*

1960 was marked by a new interest in stockings. Skirts were shorter, stockings were cheaper and dark sensual names 'golden bronze, deep honey, brown velvet, bitter chocolate' seduced the market. Women's legs suddenly seemed to have summered in the south of France giving an illusion of honeyed nudity, while the young scorned these expensive tans, and clothed their nether limbs in black or brightly coloured hose made from far heavier nylon yarn.

1963
Deceptive Decorum

Between 1960 and 1963 the
Swinging Sixties devoted to the
cult and culture of youth and their
demand for excitement, change,
equality and freedom were born.
But by 1963 this mood was still in
its infancy. The gentle silhouette of
1960 had changed almost
imperceptibly to a harder less
revealing line, bosoms were said 'to
have reluctantly retired from the
battle' but they could still just be
discerned behind loose blouse tops
and figure skimming shifts. *The
Guardian* could still write of 'a
deceptive air of decorous
demureness, a kind of inverted
modesty'.

This figure with little waist and straight almost boyish hips was not devoid of sexuality. The wish to appear desirable remained. Underclothes were covered in lace with threaded ribbon and there was increased co-ordination between coloured corsetry and lingerie. The new shades were colourful, not to say strident. 'Glory in the riot of our new coloured lingerie – Sublime, Newflame, Midnight Black, Aquablue, and Tango-orange.'

'Sophisticated Sorcery temptingly touched with lace in French Navy. Slip from a set of colour-matched lingerie in 40 denier Bri-Nylon . . . . . Price 49/11.
Washed and dried overnight.'
Advertisement

There was a fashion to place the tiny mounds of milky white breasts in uplifted scallop shells which barely covered the nipples. These delightful roundnesses owed their shape and position not to centrally placed straps but to firm underwiring and plump supporting cushions of latex foam.

'Scallop Shell Bra. Price 28/9
All colour matched in wonderful
Bri-Nylon
Wash and Dry Overnight.'
Advertisement

Stockings in Golden Tan have stretch nylon tops.

1963
Bra-Slips and Pantie-Girdle

Like the suffragettes of 1910–14 these women continued to cling to the comforting support and control of corsetry. It was too soon to let all swing free. Like the suffragettes too their dress was an odd mixture of defiance and modesty, but where the young women of 1910 had been daring without and vulnerable within, these girls merely gave the appearance of decorum in public. It was beneath the demure outercoverings that the preparations for attack in the bedroom could be seen.

The emergence of the bra slip which dispensed with that most female of garments the brassiere, revealed the need to be rid of traditional female trappings.

'In the fresh enchantment of *broderie anglaise* comes an irresistibly young piece of French ingenuity. Neither bra nor slip but both together, the bra-slip does away with messy old fashioned dressing whilst still preserving your lovely shape. Almost too pretty not to be seen the cleverly cut bra-slip has expanding straps to hold you beautifully, comfortably in place. No need to worry about unsightly slipping – that is all in the past.
Washed and dried in a trice it makes delightful sense.' *Advertisement*

'For Girls on the Move. . . .
. . . This delightful girdle really slims, whilst giving you marvellous freedom.

Whatever you're doing you'll feel perfectly comfortable with Elasti VH, now made from Lycra, an extraordinary stretch material that is strong and featherlight at the same time. This pantie-girdle gets rid of unwanted bulges: defines your shape. It follows your movements without restricting you in the least.'
Advertisement

The pantie-girdle was first introduced in the thirties but since then had been confined to sports wear. Now it was under everything.

'Bikini briefs in 40 denier Bri-Nylon. Chi-chi-chic. French Impressionist colours.' *Advertisement*

Bikinis had been around since 1956 when Bardot rocked St Tropez by appearing in two gingham frills. The minute briefs did not appear until 1960 and it took another three years before they became popular.

1965
Diana's Armour

'I am not quite a gentleman but you would hardly notice it.' Daisy Ashford, *The Young Visitors*

In 1965 trousers, for the first time, became a fashionable item of dress. Girls dressed as young men paraded the streets. This mark of the emancipated woman symbolised a kind of equality, a narrowing of the sexual difference and the beginnings of Unisex.

‘The Second Skin’
‘From America comes Moving
Control. . . . A Long-legged Panti-
roll-on in lovely lightweight Lycra.
Split crotch. Concealed Suspenders.’
Advertisement

It was important to achieve a slim
straight line. Trousers were much
tigher than they had been in the past
and therefore new forms of
foundation garments were necessary
to control wayward flesh and mould
it in a smooth straight line
particularly from waist to knee.

Stretch stockings in crimped nylon
yarn were now available.

'Lighter than light than light.'
Bri-Nylon taffeta bra with nylon
voile cups. A, B, C, cup sizes.
Price 13/11.' *Advertisement*

The brassiere ceased to be an
instrument of seduction and
emphasis was layed on its fit,
comfort and control. There was
much talk in the trade of separation
and cup sizes. It was now admitted
that girls with the same
measurements did not necessarily
have the same size breasts.

'Long legged Lycra pantie-girdle.
Ribbon rosebuds conceal
suspenders. Price £3:12:6.'
Advertisement

This was an alternative to the panti-
corselet. It was curious that girls
who appeared to all as fearless
Dianas, even Amazons, should have
crushed themselves into such
constricting garments.

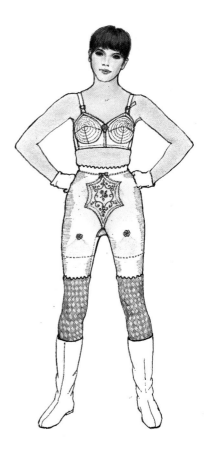

'Stretch nylon pants also in black,
white, blue and navy. Price 5/-.'
St Michael lingerie

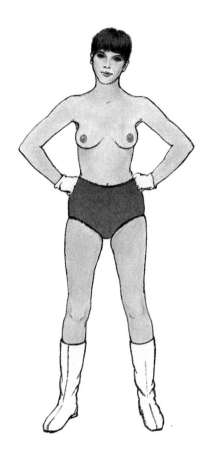

1966
Assumed Innocence

Between 1965 and 1967 the desirable figure, half Lolita, half medieval page, turned into a little girl of assumed innocence.

'. . . Tight buttoning over the high bosom which was in itself so emphasised that the effect was of 12-year-old girls wearing pre-formed bras.' *The Guardian*

But if *haute couture* was obsessed by the child French lingerie makers still regarded the woman.

Ce n'est pas seulement un soutien-
gorge de gris, de rose et de fine
dentelle.

C'est aussi et surtout un ensemble:
et un jupon dans la même nuance
romantique.
Clothes made by Lou-Boutique,
France

Underwear had occasional sorties
into romance but such moods pass.

un slip. . . . .

une porte-jarretelles

This passing phase of prettiness
served to emphasise. . . .

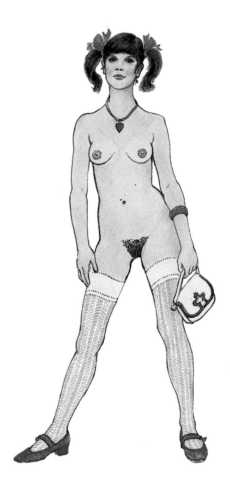

... 'a perverted innocence' in
white Alice in Wonderland
stockings.

1967
Strong Simplicity

In the sixties originality, ingenuity, enthusiasm and liberty were far more valued than sophistication, experience and classical good taste. With this came a levelling out in the matter of all clothes. It became impossible to tell a duchess from a shop girl as they were both clothed by Mary Quant above and Marks and Spencer beneath. Renowned for their permissiveness the sixties should also be remembered for the reshuffling of the class barriers.

'Stretch Bri-Nylon "Cosi-top" in jaquard design. Blue/black. Red/blue.' *St Michael lingerie*

Bri-Nylon waist slip in navy. Price 17/6.' *St Michael lingerie*

1967 saw the introduction of strongly coloured and patterned underwear whose simplicity of style had little to do with any erotic suggestion. Girls no longer needed erotic aids and with few modifications these garments would pass unnoticed on the beach or in the garden.

Matching demi-john in stretch Bri-Nylon trimmed with black lace.

The reintroduction of coloured tights and patterned stockings in the early sixties began with fairly restrained designs, but, as skirts rose, legs that were not concealed by boots became gloriously alive. When in 1967 the mini-skirt arrived and made tights essential all kinds of exuberant patterns, lacy textures, glittering weaves and rainbow colours appeared. By 1968 they had become the high fashion point of every outfit.

Three years later skirts descended; the show was over.

'All over stretch Lycra bra with nylon cups. Small cup 32–34. Medium cup 34–38. Price 17/6.'
St Michael lingerie

This brassiere proved to be the ultimate in comfort and was extremely popular. Other firms produced similar models at twice the cost.

Matching brief leg pantie-girdle with detachable suspenders.

1967
The Mini

In 1967 the distinctive silhouette
was a long pair of brightly booted
legs topped by a short flared tunic.
Since breast and waist were hidden
it was left to legs and long-lashed
lustrous eyes to proclaim femininity.

A tailored mini-slip in near nude
Bri-Nylon. Various fashion journals
echoed the newspaper lament 'All
the prettiness is gone'.

Nylon and Lycra stretch bra with fibre filled undercups. From Marks and Spencer.

Stretch briefs in nylon and Spandex.

These were not knickers but very soft little pantie-girdles made without suspenders especially for wearing over tights. These briefs were meant to be seen, rather like little girls showing their knickers.

Legs were everywhere. Girls wore gaily coloured briefs that were difficult to miss with the skirt coming only 3 or 4 inches over the thigh. Models were photographed from below with their feet wide apart. Attention was drawn to the crotch. It was the new erogenous zone.

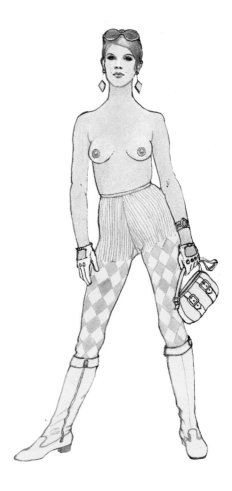

1968
The Body-Stocking

In 1968 *haute couture* produced
transparent dresses. To begin with
they were considered both shocking
and provocative but in two years
they had spread from London and
Paris to all places and men had
grown used to the phenomena. In
practice most women wore white or
semi-transparent underclothes
beneath which produced the effect
more of a naked child than a
seductively veiled woman. In spite
of all the talk of 'full-frontals',
nudity had become boring. In the
inimitable words of the advertisers,
it had been overexposed.

'. . . This time we've really come up with nothing. No Bra. No lumps and bumps to show through your dress. No buttons and bows. No straps and bones. No pushing and pulling. . . . The Body Stocking in five flesh tones.' *Advertisement*

This garment heralded in 1965 by the Rudi Geinreich 'No-Bra Bra' had an earth shattering effect on the underwear industry and the female psyche, although it never became popular. The reasons for this were simply that it left nothing to the imagination and only looked good on the beautifully young and firm, who might just as well have worn nothing.

The nipples revealed: but in practice scarcely visible beneath the outer garment, unless they were very dark and the dress very lacy.

124

If opaque white briefs were worn all darkness was obliterated. Excitement only stirred when briefs like these went on over tights.

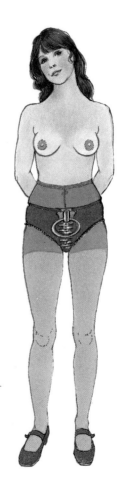

Over the last 60 years undergarments had been cast to the winds. Corsets and camisoles, combinations, petticoats, chemises and frilly drawers had all been discarded until the ultimate in no-wear underwear had been reached. But not quite – the expanses of seemingly naked flesh belonging to the 1968 girl were in actuality very decently clad. There was still one further stage to go.

It could be said that the dress of
1968 reflected society's wish to view
sexual intercourse as a wholesome
natural occupation. It also indicates
permissiveness. The naked child of
1968 had little conception of right
and wrong. This situation was too
false to last. Gradually the need to
hide behind childishness
disappeared. Nipples were either
frankly revealèd or concealed.
Women reverted to choosing their
own form of attack.

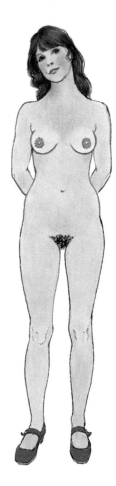

1970
See-Through Tops

In 1970 the ideal figure reached
another extreme. The androgynous
shape of Twiggy appeared whose
matchstick form made even the
flappers of the twenties seem
comparatively womanly. Perhaps, as
in the twenties, the slender form was
an expression against the normal
fecundity of women. But certainly
in the western world modern
methods of birth control were so
efficient that women had no need to
exaggerate unwilling maternalism
and curves soon made a comeback.

The see-through tops first shown in
1968, the bra burning antics of the
women's lib movement, and no-wear
underwear, produced in 1970 a
delectable collection of floating
evening dresses, whose misty muslin
transparencies, unimpaired by solid
linings were worn by the young, the
beautiful and the daring. Seduction
owed nothing to modesty. Women
chose to present their bodies
erotically veiled in diaphanous
gowns which drew direct attention
to their naked breasts.

With this emergence of frank
eroticism came the return of
deliciously pretty underwear;
garments in chiffon, *broderie
anglaise* and silk threaded through
with satin ribbon and edged with
lace, but now dresses too were made
in these materials once considered to
be the sole domain of lingerie.

1970
The Silky Trouser Suit

The trouser suit of the early
seventies was the antithesis of
masculinity. It was not designed for
androgynous Dianas, since its
purpose was to enhance the soft
rounded forms of girls who took a
delight in the sensuality of their
bodies.

Bras were not discarded everywhere, for many such a move was plain impractical. It was, however, possible to cut out that part which covered the nipples, some did.

'The Lovable Cuddle may be short but it's sweet. It won't push you together or shove you around. It's designed to cradle your bosom both gently and naturally. The Cuddle is made of Helenca stretch lace that's so pretty it seems a pity to hide it under anything. (If you want to show it off we doubt whether anyone will mind very much.) It comes in sizes 32–36. The cups fit any A or B. The price is tiny £1.15. Now honestly wouldn't you like to have the softest part of you held in a *lovable* Cuddle?. . . .
There are briefs to match too . . .'
Advertisement

Lacy knee high socks because 'Men hate tights – they're unsexy'.

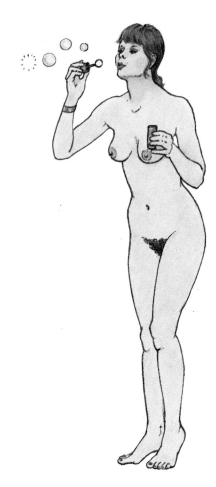

1970
A Purpose in the Bedroom

'Curves have to be in the right places.'

'. . . with longer skirts waists are definitely cinched, so bosoms have to be worn higher to prevent a pigeon-like silhouette.'

'Dotted with violets and laced with satin ribbon, a lavender petticoat in Anti-stat Celon for wearing under your most wanton Midi. Price £2.40.'
Advertisement

The tailored slip, although widely worn, was not as fashionable as it once was. The mini-mini found it a nuisance and the split midi called for something more exciting. So petticoats (slip is too quick and slippery a word for anything seductive) returned, bringing a little of their ancient glory with them.

'Pure silk Edwardian waspie and softly padded half-cup bra with underwiring in hyacinth blue trimmed with pale coffee lace and inset ribbon. Matching silk briefs.
Bra £3.60 Briefs £1.60
Waspie £7.65 '*Advertisement*

This underwear was luxurious and expensive.

'Gone are the days when a bra was no more than scaffolding to prop up your bosom. In fact gone are the days when propped-up bosoms are desirable. . . .'

'Undies are now designed to be pretty and supple and make you feel good, look good, and look sexy for your man. . . .

. . . who, we are surprised to learn, finds buying underwear for you an erotic experience.'

Finally it has been frankly admitted that underwear serves a purpose in the bedroom.

1980
T-Shirt Bra and Control Tights

By 1980 the cheerful jumble of the seventies 'dressing-up' box looks had begun to pall. Young women wanted sensible elegance and turned, not to Paris but America with its tradition of easy, streamlined, classic clothes.
Bra advertisements abounded. A new addition was the T-shirt bra with woven cups.

The modern bra now came with minimum, medium or maximum control. The trade had learnt that as well as being different in size, some breasts were floppier than others.

'Does your sweater dress let everyone know what you're wearing underneath?

The answer to VPL (visible pantie line) is a pair of control tights.
. . . smooth and comfortable and totally unlike the ghastly pantie-girdle of yesteryear. . . . Control tights give you comfort, freedom and a good fit.'

These tights belonged to a class of hosiery that had in the past only been worn by varicose vein sufferers.

1980
Cheap Central Heating

In the last few years as world energy shortages have made daily copy in the newspapers continuous central heating has become a luxury. Into this chill came Thermal Underwear and whether through wide advertising, good sense, or the jaded journalists' need for new ideas, it has assumed the form of fashion.

'To look at these hot little numbers don't exactly inflame the passions, but they are not complete turn-offs either.'

'Long sleeved fancy knit Spencer vest – cuffs and waist ribbed to give you cosy and comfortable fit in white.' *Advertisement*

'Long pants to be worn under trousers by the outdoor lady or those who need warmth all over.' *Advertisement*

Scarlet cashmere socks.

If a skirt was preferred finely knitted woollen tights in a 'rich berry colour' could be worn over briefs with their obligatory cotton gusset.

1980
Pure Luxury

Beneath the loose, layered looks of the seventies there was no need or wish for constricting corsetry; bra, briefs and tights were enough. Yet particularly towards the end of the decade there was an upsurge in luxury underwear, whose cut, fabric, (real silk and satin) and finish would not have been out of place 50 or even 70 years ago. Maybe this was a relatively inexpensive way of getting a taste of real luxury in an increasingly dreary world.

White was the favourite colour. It was said to represent Pure or Sheer luxury.

'The prettiest blooms of pure white lace and silk . . . hints of ruffles and lace – sheer luxury.' *Vogue*

Pure silk, lace trimmed camisole with pin-tucked bodice.
French knickers which feel 'frankly feminine in a way briefs never do. . .' *Good Housekeeping*

Worn with stockings that 'will have a stunning effect on your man'.

Such garments, of course, were only for high days and holidays.

1980–1
The American Line

'Clothes this season are essentially simple in fine wools, silks and cashmeres that fall and fit easily.'
Vogue

The classic American line for all its ease demanded the right kind of underclothes, 'a wardrobe of underwear to flatter and complement what went on top as well as underneath'. Fashion editors wrote articles to help their readers find the right 'underlining' which was needed for a 'smooth finish'.

'We take every care when buying a new dress so why not pay extra attention to what goes on behind the scenes.' *Good Housekeeping*

'Soft simple clothes tend to ride up when worn with no lining. Therefore it is best to wear an anti-static petticoat . . .' *Vogue*

'For glamorous evenings . . . a silky half-slip . . . a subtle and fitting addition to Warner's famous French Collection of soft beguiling underwear.' *Advertisement*

This slip has a matching 'beautiful strapless bra'.

142

While many of the sixties pantie-girdle styles were still around the newest form of corsetry was The Body Shaper, a garment like a soft, silky swimsuit, or a prettied up version of the body stocking.

One fashion journalist advised that for sheer silky dresses 'very bare underlining' was essential, but for less revealing clothes 'medium or maximum support body shapers designed on the same lines, but with re-inforced panels and moulded cups' should be chosen.

The body shaper worn over a pair of fine denier tights that boast of holding 'The Secret of Great French Dressing' 'the unique sleek fit that French women demand'.

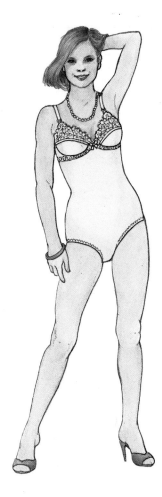

It has been said that in times of stability and certainty women wear corsets, and these are symbolic of firm moral principles. Perhaps the re-emergence of gentle corsetry like control tights and the Body Shaper in 1980 which can be seen as a hint of discipline, presages the return to firmer moral values.

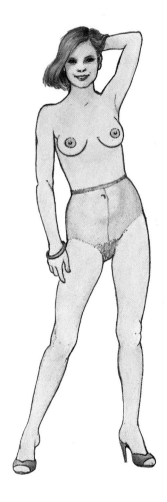